When Karma Knocks On Your Door Answer It

Linda Dianne

Copyright © 2014 by Linda Dianne

All rights reserved

No part of this book may be reproduced, stored in a retrieval system, or transmitted by any means, electronic, mechanical, photocopying, recording, or otherwise, without written permission from the author or publisher. There is one exception. Brief passages may be quoted in articles or reviews.

Library and Archives Canada Cataloguing in Publication

Cataloguing data available through Library and Archives Canada

ISBN 978-1-55483-980-3

Contents

Dedication	5
Acknowledgements	7
Introduction	9
The Dragon	14
Chapter One	
Knock, Knock! Who's there?	15
Chapter Two	
Easy Come, Easy Go	25
Chapter Three	
Saying Goodbye	
(living with grief)	35
Chapter Four	
It's MY Body, get out (cancer)	43
Chapter Five	
Working Through Mental	
Pain (guilt)	51
Chapter Six	
Strength (dealing with	
Depression)	59

Chapter Seven
   Contentment (love who
     you are)   67
Chapter Eight
   Forgiveness   79
Chapter Nine
   Life (moving forward)   87
Chapter Ten
   The Dragon and Me
   (friendship)   97
Afterword
   What colour is Karma?   105

Quotes of William Shakespeare
   used in this book   109
About the Author   111

Dedication

This book is dedicated to my son
Michael
whose love and support for me and
incredible awareness of the desires and
needs of my soul
are what makes the solid foundation
that pushes me forward and gives me
strength.

He helps me to believe in myself
and to find the strength that lies within
me.

Acknowledgements

Thank you to God who gave me the words
Knowledge and inspiration to
Write this book
(*the word inspire means "in spirit"*)

Thank you to my Spirit Guide Jooseth
Who helps guide my words and
Actions each day

Thank you to William Shakespeare for
Leaving us with
Writings of his incredible wisdom
And allowing us to continue to learn and grow
from his words

Thank you to the "dragon" which consistently
Shook my world
And helped me learn and develop my soul

Karma is for real

Introduction

What colour is Karma? What is Karma and why do I need it in my life? All good questions and I hope to answer them in a clear and concrete way, at least the way I see it and understand it to be.

Karma is simply stated as *"what goes around comes around"*. It is intentional action. A deed that is done deliberately through body, speech or mind. It is a natural law that every action produces a certain effect. Your actions no matter what they are have consequences.

Karma is neither good nor bad as it is often referred to. It is positive or negative and is the result of what you put into the universe. The law of karma is exact and states that whatever energy is sent out goes around, gathers more of the same and returns back to the sender either as positive or negative karma.

Sometimes the return of karma is instantaneous but not always. Some of us are dealing with karma from a past lifetime that we didn't deal with at that time. If you do wholesome actions, such as acts of kindness then you will experience happiness and good things will happen to you. However, if you do unwholesome actions such as hurting others then you will experience suffering. Every thought, word, feeling, action and deed that you send out into the universe will return to you. This is the law of the universe.

Karma is known as the law of <u>cause and effect</u> and its' strength is so powerful that when it comes knocking on your door you had better answer it because it is not going away.

Don't judge yourself because a lot of things happen to you and you seem to have a karma eventful life. Karma creates blocks, ties up our light and energy, and affects how we see things. Many people leave their path because they cannot deal with the challenges they encounter when karma descends. These records have to be balanced, transmuted and consumed.

Dealing with karma is good for the soul and will expand your vibrations to a higher level. We are all energy and come from the same source and as energy we vibrate. The higher vibrations you have the closer to the source you become and your soul expansion will increase. Karma is important to all of us as it is our teacher while our souls are in the human form. Soul accomplishments are the most important accomplishments you can make because when we leave our human form we return to our energy soul form which is spirit.

Dealing with karma is extremely challenging and incredibly rewarding. It is like fighting a dragon with a spoon and winning.

Chapter One
Knock, Knock! Who's There?

16 — Linda Dianne

Have you ever wondered why certain things happen to you and entertained the thought that there is the possibility that sometime, perhaps even in another life time, you may have done something to provoke karma to knock on your door?

Throughout the years many people have come and gone in my life, either through death or other changes that leave behind old acquaintances and welcome new ones. But karma has attached a tight grip on me and refuses to leave my side without the scale of *cause and effect* being balanced.

On many occasions I have entered the battlefield of the mind dealing with uncomfortable situations both in my personal and professional life. Enduring emotional abuse and hostile environments, questioning as to why I attract the very things that I detest. What the heck did I do in another life that has come back to haunt me until I make things right? Karma is knocking at my door and demanding that I take control and deal with things and move on.

There is an ancient Asian proverb that says *"When you seek vengeance, you shall dig two graves: one for the target of your vengeance, and one for yourself."* Vengeance is universally recognized to be unwise, as it is an overt, premeditated action against another person. It is an unwholesome deed resulting in unfavourable consequences.

So how do you fight karma and win? I have learned that you don't fight karma, you learn from it. It is there as your teacher helping you to realize that within your weakness lies your strength sleeping. In the times of greatest turmoil, if you use your intellect to override your emotion, you will find weakness turning into strength. Quite simply, karma can be a powerful teacher when you learn to deal with situations of all types and not just walk away from them.

Often life makes us feel impotent. We wish to do many things but feel that we are stuck. Realize that even in these times of aimless wandering, we are still learning. Sometimes life can be disappointing when reality outweighs your dreams. You can use these days to see that things that don't seem to go your way help you build patience.

I was continuously placed in situations where abuse was taking place and not always directed at me specifically but targeted at my gender which included me. I may not have abused someone in my past lives and I knew that I didn't in this life so it puzzled me as to why I attracted it. What is it that I need to learn from it? My karma was that I didn't do anything to stop the abuse instead I would, whenever I could, walk away from it. I didn't handle it. And if you don't handle Karma it will continue knocking until you do.

When I was dealing with abuse, physical and emotional, somehow I found my voice. It was hidden deep within me, and my self-esteem was at a very low point but there it was ready, armed and more powerful and determined than I had ever been. The strength within me fired up inside and with my determination I was ready to smack karma on the side of the head and shove it out the door. I wasn't taking it anymore, and it wasn't negotiable.

Despair is the feeding ground for darkness. It robs us of all hope. When there is no hope, there is no light, and the soul gives up. According to the universal law of attraction, we are what we think, so optimism dispels despair, and things immediately begin to look up. And for me they did. With my shiny untarnished spoon I was ready to beat the dragon and become the winner. My actions were pure, specific and aimed at the direct target of ending abuse on women in the workplace, in public and behind closed doors. Fear is an unresolved anxiety and it was going down with the dragon.

I identified the need for women in the Ontario government to be inspired and accepted. They needed to know that the glass ceiling was only there if you wanted it to be. I coordinated a seminar for women to speak to women of their personal journey to success and the battles they fought to be accepted. We didn't need permission we needed acceptance and respect and I was determined to fight for it and I did.

I founded the Women of Influence and Inspiration seminars for women in the public service. This was a venue where women could share personal triumphs of divorce, motherhood, abuse, sexual harassment, dealing with cancer and gaining respect in all areas of their life. These were seminars by women for women and encouraged each to follow their passion. My voice was heard, and their voices were heard and my self esteem shone with strength and power and success.

The karma I was dealing with was not abuse but self esteem and I conquered it. Low self esteem invites many unwanted demons into your life. My actions to help other women and me resulted in something good. Abuse was not going to happen to me ever again. It just wasn't welcome, invited and encouraged to stay in my life and for many women that found strength to conquer it as well. The *cause* was low self esteem, brought to my attention by abuse, and the *effect* was finding strength and power within. The dragon can sleep now and I can polish my spoon and put it away. I pushed the play button and Helen Ready began to sing "I Am Woman" and her voice loudly penetrated every room of my home while I did a victory dance.

"Our doubts are traitors, and make us lose the good we oft might win, by fearing to attempt"
– (Act I, Scene IV)

From William Shakespeare's
Measure for Measure

Chapter Two
"Easy Come, Easy Go"

The knock on the door was loud and annoying and when I opened it, there it was again, Karma staring me in the face and challenging me to another emotional battlefield. Just when life puts a smile on your heart, the dragon wags its tail and knocks you flying into a bucket of tar. Easy come, easy go for karma has the power now and I have to figure out what it is that I have to learn.

Friendships were formed throughout the years and trust was gained and then the relationships ended. Betrayal happened, trust issues took over and self doubt entered my life and wanted to stay. People have suddenly left my life that I thought were friends. There was no argument, no warning just my friends moving on and leaving me out of their life. And now they are people that I used to know.

I was feeling like a young child waving at the end of the driveway to playmates that leave for summer vacation and you get to stay home alone. As my friends little by little left my life or I left theirs without warning, without an argument or disagreement of any kind, it bothered me tremendously. Each time a friend and I parted ways I was hurt, confused and disappointed. Trust became an issue for me. Trusting my instincts, trusting anyone was an issue and the dragon was anxiously wagging its tail just waiting for a chance to swing it hard enough to send me into a self doubt reunion.

Why do people come and go so easily in and out of our lives? Why make friends when they are just going to go away and find new friendships? What does being a friend mean? To me friendship means being there for each other in happy times and sad times. The thread of life would be dark if it weren't for friends and love.

From early years to senior years making friends came easy to me. Even with my shyness I attracted people to me and learned to enjoy the many different ones that entered my life. Friends cherish each other's hopes and they are kind to each other's dreams. The Golden rule of *"do unto others as you would have them do unto you"* is the method for the culture of friendship. And yet some friendships don't last and this disrupted my life like the fierceness of death creeping around the corner and snatching them from me.

To have a good friend is one of the highest delights of life and to be a good friend is one of the noblest and sometimes the most devastating and rewarding.

I had achieved both by being a good friend and having good friends. So when they were no longer there for me the wounds inflicted upon my soul were carved deep and they hurt. As I believe that everything happens for a reason, and all that enter your life have a purpose, I began to reflect on those that I no longer connect with. Why were they in my life and why was I in theirs? And why did we suddenly part ways?

Each friend represented something new in my life that wasn't there until they arrived. As with any relationship friendships bring support and joy and occasionally strife. As I took a long look at who my friends were and who my friends are today it is amazing how different my relationship with each of them is.

Friends don't necessarily have to talk every day. They don't even need to talk for weeks. But when they do, it's like they never stopped talking. So when you are no longer connected with them there is a loss that can't been explained. Some people come into our lives and quickly go out of our lives. Some stay for a while and others for a lifetime.

Friends are not always perfect, but are always perfect for you when they enter your life and you enter theirs. Friends are a connection to life. They are the road to the past, and the road to the future. A friend accepts us as we are and helps us to be what we could be.

Self doubt was losing its strength now as my mind was letting go of the idea that I was the reason for the departure of the ones that left me. In my new found wisdom I realized that they were only supposed to be in my life and me in theirs for the learning of specific things. We were to learn from each other and when the lessons were learned moving on to new friendships would lead us to learning more. In each relationship I gave a lot and in return I received much more than I realized. Through friendship you learn to be kind, thoughtful, forgiving and you learn a different kind of love. You also learn how special you are to them and how much they mean to you. I am blessed with amazing loving friends that help me grow, pick me up when I fall and love me.

The dragon was pacing back and forth with excitement as once again my shiny spoon appeared before it and the door opened wide as it flew away. The karma wasn't about losing friends. It was about learning from each other and building relationships. My friends didn't leave my life because of me! We all just continued on our personal journeys and will probably meet again.

The *cause* was losing friends and the *effect* was learning to move forward and form new friendships and to learn more. Shining my spoon once again and putting it away feels good as I reap the benefits of dealing with karma and winning. I pushed the play button and Blake Shelton sang while I did the victory dance.

If you're alone, I'll be your shadow.
If you want to cry, I'll be your shoulder.
If you want a hug, I'll be your pillow.
If you need to be happy, I'll be your smile.
But anytime you need a friend,
I'll just be me.
~Author Unknown

Chapter Three
Saying Goodbye
(living with grief)

Bang, bang, bang was the sound coming through the walls of my home. It wouldn't stop, and the banging got louder forcing me to open the door and find out where the noise was coming from. There it was, Karma blocking my doorway with the intent to take charge of my life again. What did the dragon want this time? What is it that I didn't handle well and need to claim victory over?

I had just lost my husband and was grieving and didn't have the strength to fight the dragon and decided to ignore it. Grieving the loss of a loved one can really take over your life if you let it. But karma was in charge and wasn't going to go away. The pounding in my head joined the banging of the dragon as the tears ran down my cheeks like fountains.

Depression was settling in and I felt the tremendous weight of the death of my spouse pushing against my heart making it bleed. Grief, sadness, regret, fear, and sorrow were taking over my life and I was letting it. Grief is like a wave that floods over you and knocks you down and you feel like you are drowning. I was sinking into depression and the realization that he was really gone. Our dance together had ended and I was alone. Depression does exactly what it sounds like: it pushes you down and makes you feel immobile.

Friends and family comforted me and helped to get me through this torture that weighed heavy on my soul. There is power in hearing and talking about grief and knowing that there is no time line for grieving. We all deal with death and loss in our own time and in our own ways. By talking about grief with others and hearing their stories reminded me that we are all connected, we come from the same source and have the same spiritual DNA. They could feel my grief and know it and it was comforting.

I turn to music when my heart needs a massage of tenderness and freedom. In years gone by I constantly played Barbra Streisand songs when I wanted to dance around, fall in love, or cry. But to me the sound of jazz comforts my soul and gives me a rhythm that soothes all of me. It finds old wounds that sometimes come to surface and heals them and new ones that have festered.

The magnificent sound of the saxophone is like a magic wand to me making me come alive as the musical notes float into the universe. And when my soul was comforted I played the songs by "Pink" and belted them out to let the dragon know I was getting ready for the fight and it had better be prepared to lose.

I stopped focusing on what I had lost and how lonely I was and began to only remember and be thankful for being the one that was chosen to enjoy the free dance of life with him. I reminded myself of how loving, kind and gentle he was and the fun we enjoyed just being together. I didn't lose anything, but I gained so much. Through our time together here on earth I found true love, spiritual love, passion, and an incredible friend. I was the lucky one and there is nothing to be sad about.

He chose me to spend his final journey with and he chose me to be in his dreams, his arms and in his heart. My sadness for his leaving was now filled with so much love inside my soul that it began to shine again and I felt loved, and special and wonderful. Of course I miss him and there are days when tears flow freely but not all of them because I am sad, some are because I am overwhelmed with having the opportunity to experience so much love from just one person.

Grief is a lonely island where we feel abandoned, but we will be rescued and we will laugh, sing and dance again.

Death is only the passing from this dimension to another. Acceptance of my new life was the only way that my strength would come back. I knew that it's going to be OK, and that I would survive and my life will go on. I will have another partner to dance with and the songs in my heart will free me to enjoy the dance. Strength is nothing more than enduring life and being able to survive the heartaches and agonies we go through with our heads held high. Sometimes just walking through adversity to get to the other side is a sign of strength. And I was ready to go the distance and reach the other side with pride and confidence and as a winner.

I opened the door as wide as I could and I stood there facing the dragon with my spoon ready for the fight. The dragon leaned forward and kissed my cheek and quietly went away. I put my spoon back in the box, pushed the play button and the voice of Carrie Underwood singing "I will see you again" flooded my home as I did a victory dance.

Karma this time was about letting go, and saying goodbye, knowing that our souls will be together again and life will go on. It was about the celebration of life not the end of it. The *cause* was death and dealing with grief and the *effect* was in knowing that it wasn't goodbye, as our souls will meet again on our journey of everlasting life and love.

"*Everyone can master a grief but he that has it*".

(Act III, Scene II).

From William Shakespeare's

Much Ado About Nothing

Chapter Four
It's "MY" body, get out (cancer)

I left the medical building after having tests done to find out why my energy level was spiraling downward. I was experiencing symptoms unfamiliar to me and I wanted answers. Stress was a big contributor and grieving the loss of my husband created more stress. I was alone when the phone call came telling me that I have cancer. I had stage two uterine cancer and I needed surgery as soon as possible.

Karma was quick to take charge of my life again. The dragon was forceful this time and the news felt like I had been hit by a brick. When you are told you have cancer, the diagnosis affects not only you, but also your family and friends. You feel scared and uncertain about the unwanted changes cancer will bring to your life and theirs.

There is nothing fair about cancer and no one deserves to have it. Accepting the diagnosis and figuring out what cancer will mean in your life is challenging. My first emotion was that of shock followed by disbelief, fear, anxiety, guilt, sadness, and more. No one is ever ready to hear that they have cancer. And no one wants it.

I asked myself if I could have noticed my symptoms earlier, and wondered what I did, that may have caused cancer. I felt hopeless and sad. It was like a roadblock to a life of health and happiness. Where was the detour and how can I get to it? I found it difficult to feel positive and upbeat, especially knowing that my future was uncertain. When you are ill with this dreaded cancer your feelings need care too, just like your physical body needs care.

Pain teaches the body endurance. If allowed to, it becomes master of your life.

But this is MY body and cancer is not welcome in it and it needs to get out permanently. I'm the one in charge and the dragon is going to have a powerful fight if it is going to use cancer as a weapon to defeat me. I am strong and I am determined and I will be the winner. This is MY body and I decide what it can handle and accept. And cancer has to get out and stay out.

The dragon's tail was slapping against the door and when I opened it fire was shooting out of its mouth and it meant business. Now I have received results from more medical tests and have been advised that I have a blockage on the left side of my heart. I need surgery for cancer and now they don't know if I am strong enough to undergo it. What the heck is going on? I'm still dealing with grief, and now this. My life was now consisting of more and more medical tests and drugs and finally the doctors feel that my heart is strong enough to undergo surgery.

Prayers from friends and family and my daily talks with God was the power I had to fight cancer and get it out of my body permanently. I released anxiety with tears and music. I played sad songs so that I could cry and I played upbeat songs so that I could smile and I played love songs to feel loved. I sang, danced and cried myself to sleep and I meditated to finally bring peace to my body and mind.

I yelled at cancer and let it know that it wasn't welcome in my body and it will have to leave and never come back. This fight with the dragon was painful and difficult and there didn't seem to be a way to deal with the emotions that welled up inside of me. Cancer, how dare it take control of my life, my body and my state of mind. How dare it invite itself into my body and try to destroy me.
This is MY body and I want it back so get out, get out and stay out are the words I threw at cancer. I don't want you, nobody wants you so leave and don't come back.

This is MY body so leave me alone.

I asked God for healing, and asked him to guide the hands of the surgeons that were to remove the cancer from my body. I asked the Archangels and Jesus to be there with me to rid my body of cancer permanently. I asked the universe to destroy all signs of cancer and I called upon my spirit guide Jooseth to hold my hand and keep me safe. I prayed to all that would listen and I talked to my body to let it know what was going on. I tried everything, prayer, meditation, and had faith that I was going to beat cancer and the dragon. And I did.

Cancer is no longer in my body and I am healthy and strong again. The knock on the door was softer now, almost faint and when I opened it the dragon was there and with my shiny spoon I tapped it on the head and set it free. Victory was mine again. I pushed the play button and danced to George Michael singing "You Gotta Have Faith" as I did the Victory dance.

The karma I was dealing with was faith. Having faith in God, faith in prayer and faith in me brought cancer to a halt. Cancer was the weapon to get my attention, and faith was the cure to the suffering and healing of my body. It was time to put the spoon back in the box and enjoy my life again. The *cause* was illness in the form of cancer and the *effect* was my believing in God and the power of prayer.

"Out, dammed spot! Out, I say!" (Act V, Scene I)

From William Shakespeare's
Macbeth

Chapter Five
Working Through Mental Pain (guilt)

The sound of something hitting the door startled me and I opened it to see what had caused the noise. Karma greeted me with a grin pushed me aside and walked into my home. The dragon has left its slumber and is ready for battle.

I didn't know I loved my mother until she passed away. I never told her and this painful guilt began to control my life. I was so caught up in the fact that she never hugged me or made me feel special that I didn't realize what the impact of her absence in my life would be. Guilt is an effective state of mind in which one experiences conflict at having done something that one believes one should not have done or conversely, having not done something one believes one should have done. This is a feeling which does not go away easily.

Guilt is a spiritual killer. The only place guilt has in your life is if you did something to another person with malice. And yet I felt guilty and the pain was real. I have accepted the fact that I had to address it or it would never get beyond this pain. I had to face the truth that not only did she show no signs towards me that she loved me, I made no attempt to let her know that I loved her. It is believed that at the root of <u>false</u> guilt is the idea that what you *feel* must be true. If you *feel* guilty, you must *be* guilty.

It has been over twenty years since my mother passed away and it was time for me to deal with the guilt that sat in the pit of my stomach. Things that cannot be cured must be endured sometimes. Every hurt takes time to heal, even old wounds. It is important not to let anyone tell you that your feelings aren't real, significant, and important. They are your feelings and they are real.

As time goes by I have reflected on my life when she was in it and how it is without her. I have had the time to heal and time to allow the guilt to pass and be left in the past. In order to heal the mental pain that I carried I didn't let it define me. Sometimes life hands you difficulties from time to time. Everything, even very painful times, can be used to learn to better develop wisdom and perspective about life that will help you in the future.

In the words of William Shakespeare from Act II, Scene II of "Hamlet" *"There is nothing either good or bad, but thinking makes it so"* and my thinking she didn't love me made it so in my mind. And yet I can remember times when we laughed and drank tea together. I remember decorating cookies with her and my siblings and the stories she told to us at Halloween. I remember more of the good times now and so little of the hurtful times.

I now choose to believe that my mother had some degree of love for me and that she knew that I wanted her to love me. By wanting her love was an indirect attempt to let her know that I loved her. I no longer carry the torch of guilt and no longer feel the hurt that lingered all these years of not feeling loved by her. Guiltless minds cannot suffer. Your thoughts make things real even when it is not real *(cause and effect)*.

Life is far too precious and fragile to dedicate it to carrying past emotions that serve no purpose. Remembering what was good about our relationship mends the trail of broken dreams and helps pave the way to a better understanding of the level of love that existed. Love is a multitude of emotions and has many layers. I stopped thinking with my ego and began to think with my spirit energy and realized that love was there all the time as we come from the same source which is love. Why didn't I feel it, see it or understand that love was there between us all the time? My ego wanted the attention of being the star in her eyes but my spirit always knew that we are all perfect as spirit energy and that we are love.

With my shiny spoon ready and my mind focussed on opening the door to face the dragon, it suddenly appeared in front of me, hugged me and went away. The dragon can return to its sleep and the spoon can go back into the box. I pushed the play button and danced the victory dance while Peggy Lee sang.

The karma I was dealing with was acceptance. Learning to accept people for who they are and learning that there are many degrees of love if you are open to it. The *cause* was living without my mother's love and the *effect* was realizing that she did love me in a different way than expected and I am accepting of the fact that love has a multitude of layers.

"My salad days, when I was green in judgment."
(Act I, Scene V)

From William Shakespeare's
Antony and Cleopatra

I love you Mom

Chapter Six
Strength
(dealing with Depression)

Suddenly the door opened and a mist of cold air surrounded me and then the heavy pressure of stale air froze my body and I couldn't move. Karma had swooped into my home and caged me into a depression that I didn't see coming. The dragon was back and I had to deal with it.

Depression is an inability to function normally in everyday life. Fatigue, persistent sadness, including fits of crying easily, feelings of anxiety or emptiness all come packaged in the form of a weapon to take away your dreams and your strength. And it tried to take over my life. I found myself sleeping a lot more and experiencing unusual weight gain and yet I had a loss of appetite.

Body pains, cramps, digestive problems, headaches all go away with medication or treatment but not the mental anguish that comes with depression.

The dragon needed to be tamed and I had to find the strength to do it. I had to divert attention away from the depression. Getting rid of depression is a journey of gradual steps rather than there being a quick cure. There were times when my determination was challenged but somehow I found the strength to keep on fighting. I learned to be gentle on myself. Life isn't a race or a competition and I gave myself permission to experience sadness and then permission to experience changes and happiness.

I did research on depression and refused to associate it with me. I didn't own it, and I didn't want it. I read inspirational books and took seminars that kept me on the path to understanding how powerful our thoughts are and how to tap into my inner strength. I kicked my ego to the curb and concentrated on filling my soul with positive energy and letting my thoughts come from spirit. Spirit is being a higher life form. It is where we all came from and are learning to experience things confined in the human body. I took care of my body and ate healthy. I cut my hair and bought a new shade of lipstick. I played my pick- me- up song "Footloose" by Kenny Loggins over and over again. I watched movies that gave women power, romance and love. I cleaned out closets and rearranged things in my home. And I meditated daily.

Remembering that misery loves company, I decided to be around positive people. I changed my behaviour first by changing my thoughts. I was worth fighting for. I monitored my thoughts and learned to recognize the feelings I experienced with each thought. When my thoughts were judgemental and negative they were coming from my ego and when they came from spirit they were positive, loving and pure. A bad day for the ego is a good day for the soul.

The difference between self esteem and self compassion is that you judge and assess yourself against others comparing your life with theirs and in the end lowers your self esteem, which is what you feel and think about yourself. Self compassion is all about being kind, loving and respectful to you. I forgot how important this was to my soul and my energy.

Doing fun things by myself and treating me to a night out alone were new challenges for me and I continued to help others. I took time to congratulate myself on my accomplishments and I even read my first published book "Hugs From Heaven" to remind me of who I am and how strong I am. I told the truth to myself and didn't deny how I felt and how my body felt. When you argue with reality you will lose 100% of the time.

The heavy stale air that froze me into the depression cage was gone now and my soul felt the freedom it had longed for. With my shiny spoon in hand I faced the dragon which tilted its head, turned slowly and went away.

The karma I was dealing with this time was in believing that I am strong and have the strength and the tools to accomplish many things. We all need to believe, reach out to the people that matter to us and give permission to ourselves to experience life and the changes that come with it. Living is a journey and it can be all that you want it to be. Believe in yourself, you are special, powerful, strong, beautiful and loved.

The *cause* was depression and the *effect* was belief in having the tools to move forward on my journey and knowing that I had the power and strength to conquer all obstacles in my way. I learned to love me not just the way I am but also because of who I am.

I pushed the play button and danced the victory dance to Billy Gilman singing "Little Bitty Pretty One" and ended the day with a smile.

"Though she be but little, she is fierce!"
(Act III, Scene II)
From William Shakespeare's
A Midsummer Night's Dream

Chapter Seven
Contentment
(love who you are)

I woke suddenly to an unfamiliar sound and queasiness settled in my stomach. I began to cry and loneliness snuggled around me keeping me prisoner in my bed. The sound became louder and the queasiness stronger as I freed myself from the confines of the bedroom. What is this, what is going on and why now?

Sliding my feet into my slippers and making my way to the kitchen I heard a thump at my door. As I slid the door open I was face to face with Karma. What now? Why was Karma knocking at my door and surrounding me with sadness and discontent? Haven't I dealt with enough? Why is the dragon so eager to penetrate my life and take power over me?

I wanted to cry and I needed to cry in order to release the loneliness that was in my thoughts. Being suddenly single and moving forward after a long beautiful loving relationship is a challenge. There were times when loneliness took over and even the power to love myself was taken away. How do you pick yourself up and be ready to give and receive love again? Where do you start? Will love be in your future and will you let it in?

I had to learn to be happy being me! Being confident about who I am and recognizing what I loved about myself was the beginning. The dragon wasn't going to take over my life and make me feel unloved and unwanted. My spoon was ready and the dragon would soon know who I am and my power.

To help me recognize what is good about me I focused first on the type of compliments that I had received through the years. I began to appreciate what makes me unique among my friends and family and what makes them unique to me. Everyone is insecure about something and I needed to minimize my insecurities. Recognizing and accepting my flaws and learning to laugh at myself seemed to smooth the path that I was travelling on.

Nobody's perfect, so why was I thinking that I needed to be? What is perfection anyway? Perfection is in loving yourself just the way you are. Perfection is being in a loving state. It is kindness, gentleness and respectful. Perfection is never forgetting to laugh and to leave time for laughter each day of your life. It is also forgiveness, not just saying the words but being forgiving.

The dragon was definitely not going to win this battle. I began to push my insecurities aside and focus on my favourite features. I tried to see what others may see in me and told myself that what I thought were flaws were only noticed by me and invisible to others.

Recognizing that I needed to transform myself from the inside out I focused on the fact that we are all a soul family. Riding the wave of life without the knowledge and wisdom of the needs of our soul cannot be done successfully. Personal growth in all areas of our life is important and I was just focussing on my feelings which limited my growing. When you only focus on parts of you it is like having bends in the light ahead with no clear direction to follow.

To master control of my life I needed to shift from the inside out and to do that my thinking had to change. I had to update my thoughts and make sure that they were mine and not something forced on me. You can't fake vibrations therefore positive thinking was not enough I had to be in the state of positivity which is love, compassion, forgiveness and respect. I removed the static and confusion from my thoughts and focused on understanding the principles of energy. After all I was energy so it made sense to know something about it.

Dealing with the human form is challenging for our souls to enjoy the freedom that exists when they are not confined. Understanding that certain things or people will contract or expand our energy and affect our vibrations helped me to make an attitude change. I was always living in the fast forward mode and have changed to living in the now mode. To change my attitude about certain things and the way I live my life, was easier than I thought it would be. I realized that the voice of the ego shouts and is demanding and the voice of wisdom, which I now have learned to listen to, doesn't shout, instead it whispers forcing me to listen.

I thought of the people in my life and identified the changes taking place in my body as I focused on each person individually. My energy levels changed in different degrees of contraction and uneasiness with some and expansion with others. With the change in my energy from contraction to expansion my vibrations also changed. When my energy contracted my vibrations were slow and somewhat faint and my emotions and thoughts were of sadness, hurt, despair and negative. When my energy expanded my vibrations were spinning like a child's wind- up toy and my emotions and thoughts were happy, loving, compassionate and positive.

Love is the highest of all vibrations and is the truth among all energy and cannot be faked. When love is your highest thought and you are in the state of love, giving and receiving it your vibrations expand like an inverted pyramid gradually spreading and widening the area around you. You cannot fake your vibration credibility. Thinking positive thoughts are not enough, you need to be positive.

I needed to get out of my own way and get to know myself. Your relationship with yourself is also the relationship that shapes how you experience life. I asked myself who am I when no one is looking? Do I really run my own race? I gave myself permission to make mistakes. My motto is *"you don't need a title to be important, you already are"* and I was finally letting myself live the words I spoke. You can't get to courage without going through vulnerability and I needed to start saying yes to myself and stop saying no.

I began to love my wardrobe, after all I chose everything in it and I donated the clothes I no longer felt comfortable wearing. I shopped in my own closet and learned more about me through my selection of colours and styles. I began to know, like and understand who I am.

Carving out some "me time" everyday was now a routine and knowing when I needed a change from routine became second nature to me. I learned to be happy with the people in my life and gained more happiness through the friendships I made. I am happy with where I live and love the neighbourhood. I learned to accept an apology and move beyond the hurt. Learning to forgive is like performing a miracle. When you forgive and let go of the pain and hurt associated with the need to forgive, your heart opens to receive an abundance of love.

I attended an "I Can Do It" conference and met Anita Moorjani, one of the keynote speakers. Anita talked about her journey from cancer, to near death and to true healing. She talked about her near death experience and wrote about her journey in a book entitled "Dying To Be Me". Her incredible experience, wisdom, faith and strength resonated with me to a high degree and helped me appreciate my own battle with cancer and how beautiful my life is. I am not "dying to be me" I am "living to be me" and honoured to do so.

I learned that I am happy being me and embrace this amazing opportunity to be the best me that I can be, because I am the only one that can do that. Learning to honour myself and the amazing accomplishments of my soul gives me the strength to run my own race and focus on my own knowing that I am safe, strong and of the divine source.

My spoon is in my hand and the door is open and I am face to face with the dragon which just smiles, give's a wink and flies away. The spoon is now safely in the box and the smile on my face and in my heart is beautiful.

The Karma I was dealing with is contentment and gratitude. Loneliness was the weapon to *cause* me to learn to love myself and the *effect* was the incredible journey into my soul and finding out who I am and loving me. I now dedicate my life to really living and enjoying it until I die and return home to the spirit world.

My ego has been kicked to the curb and hopefully at its final resting place because I am now in control and my hands are on the steering wheel as my journey continues.

I pushed the play button and while the Beatles sang "All You Need Is Love" I danced the victory dance.

"This above all: to thine own self be true"
(Act I, Scene III)

From William Shakespeare's
Hamlet

Chapter Eight
Forgiveness

The door to my condo flew open as if a sudden fierce wind had forced it. It startled me at first until I recognized the almighty Karma standing boldly in the doorway. The dragon was back!

I found myself trying to cope with being accused of something that I didn't do or know anything about. It puzzled me that "a friend" could be so spiteful and so accusatory towards me. I had been hurt before by the actions of others towards me but this was different. How could someone that I trusted turn on me in a split second without truth being part of the equation. How do I deal with this, and how do I forgive them?

Forgiveness is the intentional and voluntary process by which a victim undergoes a change in feelings and attitude regarding an offense and lets go of negative emotions such as vengefulness. It is a form of reconciliation, a restoration of a relationship.

As a psychological concept, the benefits of forgiveness have been explored in religious thought, the social sciences and medicine. It may be considered simply in terms of the person who forgives including forgiving themselves, in terms of the person forgiven or in terms of the relationship of the forgiver and person forgiven.

I needed to forgive "my friend" and forgive myself for believing that they were a friend. I started this process by asking God to forgive them and to help them find and accept the truth. I was deeply hurt, and struggling to deal with the harshness of the sharp words that were thrown at me as I was being accused of a wrong doing that I had no knowledge of. I was their friend and would never intentionally hurt anyone so how could they turn on me with such hatred? How did they so easily turn from friend to being foe?

I prayed for guidance and strength to forgive and I continually asked God to forgive them and guide them to the truth. We all make mistakes and people get hurt but bouncing back from deep wounds isn't easy. Even though I prayed for guidance and strength I still had to do it. I had to accept that our friendship will never be the same and I had to look deep within my soul to find out why they would think so little of me. What did I do to bring on such a change in someone I liked and trusted?

I decided to be compassionate with myself. I was riding a wave that was dangerous to my health, and outlook on life. I knew the truth and believed that soon they would know it and will have to forgive themselves and ask for my forgiveness.

I gave myself permission to untie the bindings and loosen myself from that person that had tied me to the pain I was experiencing. I chose to forgive them and I did. Forgiveness is not acceptance of wrong behaviour. I also decided to not spend anymore energy on the incident because negativity is depressing spiritually and emotionally and it wasn't worth the pain that was inflicted upon me. I had better things to do with my time.

Forgiveness comes easy when you know what you say or do is about them, it's not about you. Forgiveness is a choice and it is a powerful choice to make. I needed to practice forgiveness and be forgiving not letting the pain and hurt affect me. You can apologize with words, but your actions are more powerful and not letting someone else's mistake affect me was the only way for me to move forward. Their mistake was their mistake not mine and the truth would prevail and karma will knock at their door and wait for them to answer it.

When the phone call came and the voice on the other end spoke my name and asked forgiveness of me, my prayers were answered. The truth was out and facing my accuser. The apology was accepted, and forgiveness was also. Our friendship will continue but perhaps not as strong and trust in this friendship will take time.

The dragon was sitting comfortably on my doorstep nodding its head up and down as if saying I told you so. I took out my spoon and presented it with ease of a swordsman to the dragon which backed away gracefully and left. My spoon now safely in its box and my vibrations flowing with love and gratitude for once again claiming victory over the dragon, I felt content.

The Karma I was dealing with was forgiveness. I needed to learn to forgive the actions of others towards me and to forgive myself in order to move forward. The *cause* was being wrongfully accused and the *effect* was learning the value of forgiveness and letting go of pain and hurt. I pushed the play button and Keith Urban sang while I did the Victory dance.

"what's done is done"
(Act I, Scene I)
From William Shakespeare's
Macbeth

Chapter Nine
Life
(moving forward)

I was sitting quietly in my living room thinking about the choices I have made and where they have taken me when I heard a knock on my door. I opened it slowly and carefully only to find Karma standing in front of me. Again the dragon was in my face taking up residence in my head and forcing this peacefulness I was enjoying to come to an end. How dare the dragon just pop in and out of my life without warning!

I was moving forward in my life and reflecting on my past journey to avoid the mistakes made and to focus on the lessons I learned. Too many people today are stuck in their past memories blocking an incredible journey that lies ahead of them. Living in the past to me is just a waste of time. There is no future in the past and so much to gain by leaving it behind. The only way to move forward is to motivate yourself to quit looking back. Thinking about your road of life that is still ahead of you and knowing that you can live it with happiness and love will reward you in so many ways. If you are always looking in the past than you will never live the incredible life and enjoy the wonderful journey that you are meant to have.

My journey thus far has been filled with tragedy, disappointments, confusion, sadness, betrayal, both physical and emotional illness and pain, but I have learned to kick it all to the curb. There is no room whatsoever for any of it on this next portion of my journey. This part of my life is about me, and for me. It is filled with love, friendship, respect, forgiving and giving.

My new journey began when I defeated cancer and took charge of my thoughts and my body. I am strong, healthy, happy and determined to let my spirit be free to experience life as it should be. I know that better things are ahead and the transition from the past to the present is challenging and rewarding. I closed the door to my past by writing my first book "Hugs From Heaven" where I shared parts of my life that I felt necessary to share and to bury for eternity.

I believe that nothing happens by accident and there are no coincidences. I know that there is only going to be one day at a time and one moment at a time and each day will be different in some way but each day will also be precious because I have lived it. There are seasons for everything in nature and there are seasons for everything that is in your life. What is now doesn't last forever, only love does.

To move forward I needed motivation, a positive attitude, to be open to new things in life and self respect. It is easy to run through the maze of life without pausing to think of its meaning. And it is just as easy to just exist without giving your life a purpose and enjoying it to the fullest. I chose to live a more meaningful life focused on the things that I do, and enjoy. I question if what I'm doing matters. More importantly does it matter to me?

Realizing and feeling that what you are doing has a real purpose and meaning that matters to you will make a huge difference in your life and those that are in it. I have learned to relax more and not take things so seriously. Each day I try to identify what is important for me to do that day and what I can accomplish.

I have also dedicated time to pursue my passion of writing, meeting friends for lunch, travelling and enjoying the wonderful afternoon tea ceremonies with special friends. Each time I do something I love, it creates joy inside me and my vibrations are strong and powerful.

Every time I make a choice, a decision or a gesture I am aware of what I am sending out into the universe. It is important to have self awareness. I am mindful of what I do at all times, and I make sure that I am living my life according to my principles. It is important to review your actions each day, taking stock of those that may have strayed from your path. It is necessary to work towards correcting any incidents in the future by answering the door when karma knocks on it.

I choose to live with compassion both for me and for others. To quote the Dalai Lama *"One must be compassionate to one's self before external compassion"*. I enjoy the rewards of helping others through my psychic strengths and gifts. It is like giving back to the universe and for me helping others in anyway gives my life more meaning and purpose.

Learning to simplify my life took time and I'm not sure that it is completely there yet but my life is filled with happiness and many blessings. I choose not to let the little things bother me. I accept other's opinions as simply that it is their opinion and they are entitled to it and I don't place opinions of others with more value than mine. When you allow someone else's opinion to outweigh yours and you are feeling hurt than you are thinking with your ego. Different opinions are important and will help you look at things in a broader way. Gaining control of my life and understanding that I was always in charge of it, even when I thought I wasn't, lessens the stress I carried that was weighing me down.

Life can be beautiful, loving and fulfilling if you just give it a chance and be open to just being the wonderful, loving soul that you are. Let your vibrations always be strong and filled with joy, love and kindness. When your inner light shines both you and the universe will light up the hearts of others with a smile that will linger for a while. Being true to yourself and loving yourself is the key to a beautiful life and a gentle caring soul.

The karma I was dealing with was life. I accepted all the challenges that came with learning, and knowing that moving forward is rewarding and necessary to enjoy a happy and loving life here on earth. The *cause* was reflecting on past memories and making them part of my future, and the *effect* was letting them go and only looking forward knowing the best is yet to come.

The dragon was standing at my door with its eyes beaming with pride as if it had just won the battle. But with my shiny spoon held in front of it, reflections of the past were no longer there, and the dragon gracefully went away. Now the spoon is back in the box and I pushed the play button where "Pink" sang loudly and I did a victory dance.

"For ever and a day"
(Act IV, Scene I)
From William Shakespeare's
As You Like It

Chapter Ten
The Dragon and Me
(friendship)

I was sitting calmly on a bench in a little park that is close to my home. My thoughts were focused on how life can deal out blows and leave us discouraged, frustrated, depressed and drained but we always bounce back. The sound of an ice cream truck broke my train of thought as it blew whistles and played musical tunes to announce it being there.

Children seem to come out of nowhere and circled around the truck choosing their favourite treat. Suddenly I wasn't alone, as the bench jolted to the impact of someone or something taking up space at the other end of the bench that I was sitting on. It was the dragon. My spoon was not with me and I tried not to show fear. The dragon just smiled and sat there calmly with me enjoying the rays of sunlight that filtered through the trees. The dragon had become my friend.

When you rely on the power of replacing negative thoughts with positive ones you fail to see the point of something any longer. There was no need for me at any time to fear the dragon and yet I did. There was no need to doubt myself but at times I did. There was no need to hold onto hurt and pain from the past or at anytime but I did. There was no need to feel insecure but I did. There was no need for me to feel unloved and unwanted but I did.

I took charge of my thoughts before they filtered into the universe. I acknowledged that it is just negative thinking and not what was destined for me. They were simply a set of bad thoughts that served no real importance to me but harm. The secret is to believe in yourself, pick yourself up, dust yourself off and start all over again by changing your thoughts to positive ones and being positive.

I reached over and touched the dragon to let it know that there is no fear between us just friendship. I wanted to thank it for helping me to take strength when dealing with the challenges that karma had put to me. All that the dragon and I had been through together helped to strengthen my resolve to improve my approach and strengthen my ability to bounce back. Dealing with difficult moments changes us for the better.

When hurt and pain land at your doorstep you can step over it and try to ignore it or you can deal with it so that it is gone forever. Each soul learns and grows through the physical, emotional, intellectual and spiritual levels of karmic evolution. We all evolve from getting even to righting our wrongs, and from changing others to improving our own physical and emotional balance.

As souls evolve, there are different ways of balancing karma. Karma is not a penance, but an opportunity to evolve. I needed to own that I had created the karmic events that were brought to me to deal with. Once I recognized my life's lesson each time the dragon appeared all I needed to do was forgive myself, ask for forgiveness, guidance and strength to balance karma. Nothing changes until you do and you are the only one that can change you.

It is very important to respect the spiritual side of your life and to take a break. Allow yourself to laugh more. Laughter is said to be like inner jogging and it makes you feel great all over. Take time to enjoy the "play" in your life and enjoy the work in your life. There is no path to happiness you need to find the happiness within you.

I am who I am today because of all that I have been through and dealt with. I am friends with karma and my soul has evolved. Many lessons have been learned and I feel good about life and how wonderful it can be by changing my thinking and being aware of the universal law of *"cause and effect"*.

I have learned the value and miracle of loving yourself always and getting to know who you are and what you are. I have learned the incredible art of forgiveness and throwing away the pain and hurt associated with the reasons that forgiveness was needed. I have learned about the wonderfulness of friends both being one and having them in my life. I have dealt with grief and loneliness and have learned to heal my heart and strengthen my belief in God. I have dealt with depression and learned to get out of my own way and move forward.

I look forward to the visits from the dragon and keep my spoon ready just in case the dragon springs upon me with a stronger force than expected. I look forward to dancing with a new partner and sharing my dreams with them and being part of their dreams. I look forward to the new songs in my heart and the freedom to just live and enjoy each moment.

I pushed the play button and the crooning voice of Paul McCartney sang

"Let it Be", as I sat in solitude reflecting on the path that is leading me forward to experience love once again. I am ready for the dance!

"All the world's a stage, and all the men and women merely players. They have their exits and their entrances: And one man in his time plays many parts"

(Act II, Scene VII)
From William Shakespeare's
As You Like It

Afterword
What colour is Karma?

For me the colour of Karma is pink. It used to be black until I accepted it as a learning tool. I welcome the challenges of the dragon now and like a sleuth solving the mystery put before me, I delight in conquering the dragon with my shiny spoon.

So when Karma knocks on your door
Answer it
because it is not going away
and it is your friend.

The universal law of "Cause and Effect"

Quotes of William Shakespeare used in this book

1. "Our doubts are traitors, and make us lose the good we oft might win, by fearing to attempt"
    (Act I, Scene IV) *Measure for Measure*

2. "Everyone can master a grief but he that has it".
    (Act III, Scene II) *Much Ado About Nothing*

3. "Out, dammed spot! Out, I say!"
    (Act V, Scene I) *Macbeth*

4. "My salad days, when I was green in judgment."
    (Act I, Scene V) *Antony and Cleopatra*

5. *"Though she be but little, she is fierce!"*
   (Act III, Scene II) *A Midsummer Night's Dream*

6. *"This above all: to thine own self be true"*
   (Act I, Scene III) *Hamlet*

7. *"what's done is done"*
   (Act I, Scene I) *Macbeth*

8. *"For ever and a day"*
   (Act IV, Scene I) *As You Like It*

9. *"There is nothing either good or bad, but thinking makes it so"*
   (Act II, Scene II) *Hamlet*

10. *"All the world's a stage, and all the men and women merely players.*
    They have their exits and their entrances: And one man in his time plays many parts"

   (Act II, Scene VII) *As You Like It*

About the Author
Linda Dianne

Linda Dianne is an Author, Psychic, Certified Hypnotist, Certified Angel Card Reader, networking specialist and inspirational speaker.

After serving 25 years in the Ontario Public Service (OPS), Linda retired on July 1, 2010 to pursue her passion of helping people in a more personal way through psychic readings and hypnotherapy.

During her career in the OPS she held several positions and worked in five different ministries.

In 2001, Linda developed and coordinated the first inspirational seminar for Women in the OPS and was the OPS Coordinator for the Women of Influence and Inspiration Seminars. In 2006 she received an Amethyst Award for her outstanding achievement as the Founder of the Women of Influence and Inspiration Seminars. She is also the recipient of the Spirit of Recognition Citation for her personal commitment, long standing support and significant contribution to the employee recognition program and received a certificate of recognition for being nominated for a Valuing People Award. Linda has also been nominated twice for a Woman of Distinction Award.

As an inspirational speaker and cancer survivor, Linda talks about her life and enlightens the audience on the use of colour and the energy that surrounds each of us.

Linda has been featured in the Women's Post and in a government magazine called Topical.

Her motto is "You don't need a title to be important you already are" which is featured in the 2014 Woman's Advantage Shared Wisdom Calendar that is distributed worldwide.

Other books written by the Author are:

Hugs from Heaven (Divine Intervention)
A story of her personal journey to unconditional love, comfort and forgiveness and peace.

Strange Normal (Journey of a Psychic)
A story of her personal journey as a psychic sharing her experiences and communication with "the other side"

www.ingramcontent.com/pod-product-compliance
Lightning Source LLC
Chambersburg PA
CBHW052101070526
44584CB00017B/2277